GENETIC CONDITIONS

Down Syndrome

PETRA MILLER

Cavendish Square

New York

Published in 2016 by Cavendish Square Publishing, LLC
243 5th Avenue, Suite 136, New York, NY 10016

Copyright © 2016 by Cavendish Square Publishing, LLC

First Edition

Website: cavendishsq.com

This publication represents the opinions and views of the author based on his or her personal experience, knowledge, and research. The information in this book serves as a general guide only. The author and publisher have used their best efforts in preparing this book and disclaim liability rising directly or indirectly from the use and application of this book.

CPSIA Compliance Information: Batch #CW16CSQ

All websites were available and accurate when this book was sent to press.

Library of Congress Cataloging-in-Publication Data

Miller, Petra, author.
Down syndrome / Petra Miller.
pages cm. — (Genetic conditions)
Includes bibliographical references and index.
ISBN 978-1-5026-0938-0 (hardcover) ISBN 978-1-5026-0939-7 (ebook)
1. Down syndrome. I. Title.
RC571.M55 2016
616.85'8842—dc23

2015023056

Editorial Director: David McNamara
Editor: Fletcher Doyle
Copy Editor: Nathan Heidelberger
Art Director: Jeffrey Talbot
Designer: Alan Sliwinski
Senior Production Manager: Jennifer Ryder-Talbot
Production Editor: Renni Johnson
Photo Research: J8 Media

The photographs in this book are used by permission and through the courtesy of: Rachel Frank/Fuse/Getty Images, cover; Monkey Business Images/Shutterstock.com, 5; John Minihan/Evening Standard/Hulton/Getty Images, 8; Don Mason/Blend Images/Getty Images, 11; DeAgostini/Getty Images, 13; Hulton Archive/Getty Images, 16; Biophoto Associates/Science Source/Getty Images, 18; Bob Thomas/Popperfoto/Getty Images, 20; Snapgalleria/Shutterstock.com, 22, 24; FOX via Getty Images, 31; United News/Popperfoto/Getty Images, 32; BSIP/UIG via Getty Images, 34; Monkey Business Images/Shutterstock.com, 38; AP Photo/Chris O'Meara, 41; Monkey Business Images/Shutterstock.com, 43; Eleonora_os/Shutterstock.com, 47; Jovan Mandic/Shutterstock.com, 50; CDC/Dr. Clark Heath, 53; Ttsv/iStock/Thinkstock, 54.

Printed in the United States of America

CONTENTS

Introduction

The way in which society treats people with Down syndrome has changed drastically in the last sixty years. Children with the condition are raised at home instead of in institutions. They sometimes attend public schools. When they graduate, they live on their own and find jobs.

The move into the mainstream of life has made people with Down syndrome much more visible. You have probably seen a child or grown-up with Down syndrome, a **genetic disorder** that affects physical and mental development. Because it shows up in outward features such as the shape of the face and the head, people with Down syndrome are easy to recognize. Teenagers and adults with Down syndrome tend to be short and heavy, with the backs of their heads somewhat flattened. Vision problems are common, and many children with Down syndrome have eyes that aren't aligned properly. Also, they share an assortment of health problems, such as serious heart defects.

The British physician John Langdon Down (1828–1896), who described the syndrome in 1866, wrote that "when placed

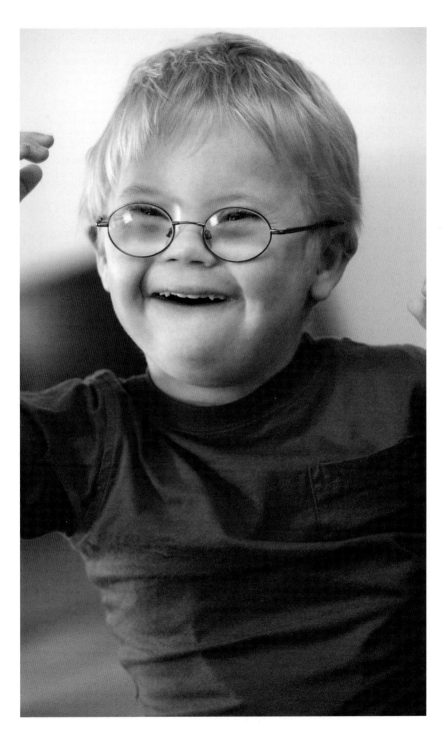

Children with Down syndrome can be identified by the alignment of their eyes and the shape of their heads, but they are also usually happy and gentle.

Introduction

side by side," people with Down syndrome look like "members of the same family." To a degree, this is true. But, of course, people with Down syndrome also resemble members of their own families.

There are mental and emotional similarities among people with Down syndrome as well. Although some people with the disorder have intelligence within the normal range, most have some intellectual disabilities. Both children and adults with Down syndrome tend to be happy, gentle, friendly, and affectionate.

Down syndrome is caused by an error in the copying of genetic material when it is passed from parents to their offspring. As a result of a genetic error, people with Down syndrome have an extra copy of a **chromosome** in many or all of their body cells. To learn more about this disorder, scientists have had to unlock some of the deepest mysteries of life.

Among these mysteries is how cells divide for reproduction so the mother and father each can contribute half of the child's genetic material. Once this was learned, understanding of this genetic disorder grew rapidly. This is the story of the ongoing search for answers to this genetic puzzle and of the changes in the lives of people living with Down syndrome.

Chapter One

Right and Wrong

P eople who try to advance our knowledge of science can make great discoveries, and they can make great errors. John Langdon Down, the scientist who described the disorder that now bears his name, did both.

In the 1860s, physicians and biologists were excited about Charles Darwin's theory of evolution. Darwin (1809–1882) presented evidence that all living things, including human beings, had evolved from earlier forms of life on Earth. A popular scientific theory linked to Darwin's ideas was that people suffering from some disorders were "throwbacks" to earlier stages in human development.

In 1866, Down published a scientific paper entitled "Observations on an Ethnic Classification of Idiots." At the time, "idiot" was used as a medical label for people with severe

Normansfield Hospital, in Middlesex in the United Kingdom, was founded by John Langdon Down. It is now the headquarters of the Down's Syndrome Association.

intellectual disabilities. In his paper, Down suggested that what he called **mongolism** was an example of a backward evolution, or retrogression, probably to some common ancestor of present-day Asians and Europeans. The terms "Mongol" and "Mongoloid" were words that Europeans used to designate the peoples of Asia. The slanting eyes and relatively flat faces of the patients Down examined suggested to Down a likeness between them and what he called in his paper the "great Mongol race."

Although Down's theory of retrogression was incorrect, it did contain a hint of the real cause of the disorder. Down recognized that his patients suffered from problems related to

Down Syndrome

heredity, the biological process by which physical and mental characteristics are passed on from one generation to the next. In other words, in a time before the discovery of **genes** or chromosomes, Down was correct in guessing that the syndrome was what we now call a genetic disease.

SEARCHING FOR ANSWERS

Correctly identifying a disorder is a crucial step in finding its causes and its treatment. Down deserves credit for making that crucial first step.

Down was an Englishman who had a scientific mind. In 1858, he was appointed medical superintendent of the Royal Earlswood Asylum for Idiots in Surrey. Down made many observations about the patients in his care. These observations led to his 1866 paper, in which he identified a set of patients at the hospital who bore similar physical and mental characteristics—the indicators of what we now call Down syndrome.

During the late nineteenth and early twentieth centuries, medical scientists learned a great deal about people with Down syndrome and their special medical problems but relatively little about the cause of the disorder. Since evidence was scarce, there were many theories.

Physicians noticed that older women were more likely to have a child with Down syndrome. Perhaps, some speculated, this was due to older mothers' exhaustion after a long series of pregnancies. Now we know that an older mother is more likely to have a baby with Down syndrome regardless of whether she has previously given birth.

Name Change

The inaccurate terms "mongolism" and "mongoloid" were attached to the condition described by John Langdon Down for about one hundred years. There are many reasons why those terms were eventually dropped. One was the discrediting of the popular notion among Europeans of the racial superiority of Caucasians. Also, most medical authorities realized fairly quickly that the resemblances between the so-called mongoloids and Asian people were very superficial. Patients with Down syndrome were found among people of Asian and African descent as well as among Europeans.

Embarrassment was probably the reason why the scientific community started referring to the condition as "Down syndrome" in the 1960s. In a letter to the British medical journal *Lancet*, nineteen scientists complained that "the increasing participation of Chinese and Japanese investigators in the study of the condition imposes on them the use of an embarrassing term." *Lancet* editors dropped the offensive terms in 1964, and the World Health Organization followed in 1965.

In 1966, researchers gathered in London to commemorate the one-hundredth anniversary of Down's paper. In a discussion of the condition's name, a Dr. Matsunaga said: "I am not happy with the words mongol, mongolism and mongoloid ... The basic question is this: is it ever justified in medical terminology to misapply a name, especially a geographical one, to a disease when this name becomes inappropriate because of increased understanding of the underlying **pathology**?"

By the 1970s, the offensive terms were no longer in use.

Physicians and scientists wrongly theorized that tuberculosis in the mother, alcoholism, thyroid deficiencies, mental or emotional stress during pregnancy, or a virus might cause Down syndrome.

TWIN CLUES

Gradually, more attention became focused on the likelihood that the disorder was genetic—related to biological inheritance. There was some evidence that the disorder ran in families.

The presence of Down syndrome in identical twins provided a clue that the condition is inherited.

As more cases were found, scientists began to notice that in monozygotic twins (so-called identical twins born from the splitting of one fertilized egg), both or neither had Down syndrome. However, among dizygotic twins (fraternal twins, from two fertilized eggs), in only a few cases did both twins have the disorder. The same thing that made twins identical—their genetic inheritance—gave them both Down syndrome. This evidence further suggested that the disease was genetic and not caused by an event like the mother catching a virus during her pregnancy.

Breakthrough

Petrus Waardenburg hypothesizes in 1932 that nondisjunction, the failure of a pair of chromosomes to separate during meiosis, causes Down syndrome.

By the 1930s, scientists knew that the blueprint for the human body was contained in packets of information found in the nucleus of every cell of the body. They called the information genes, though at that point the chemical nature of genes was unknown. They knew that the genes were bundled in structures called chromosomes, which were observable under microscopes.

CHROMOSOMES

In the early twentieth century, scientists did extensive research on the fruit fly, a creature convenient for genetic research because it reproduces every day and has large and relatively simple chromosomes. Through these studies, a great deal was learned about how chromosomes are involved in reproduction.

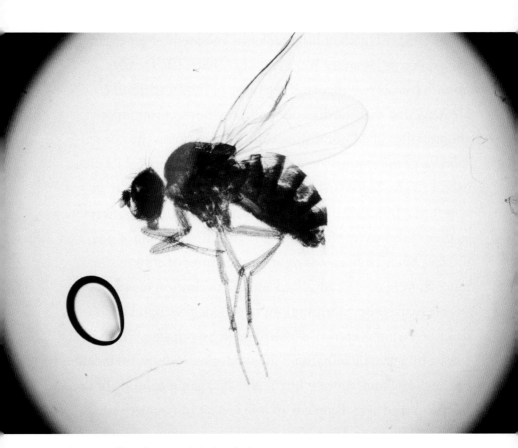

The study of fruit flies provided a lot of information on genetics.

Scientists knew that chromosomes came in pairs and that during reproduction each parent contributed half of his or her chromosomes to the child. They knew that normal human beings had around forty-six chromosomes. They also knew that errors at the chromosome level sometimes occurred during reproduction. Usually the offspring whose genetic material carried such errors did not survive, but sometimes they did. Scientists began to think that some illnesses might result from such errors.

In 1932, a Dutch ophthalmologist and medical geneticist named Petrus Johannes Waardenburg (1886–1979) came up with the correct theory of the cause of Down syndrome. He suggested that the disorder was caused by a chromosome abnormality called **nondisjunction**. Disjunction is the normal splitting of the chromosome pairs, the function that enables each parent to give half of his or her chromosomes to the child. In nondisjunction, one pair of chromosomes fails to split correctly, so the child ends up with either an extra chromosome or one too few. Waardenburg was right, but the tools of chromosome research were not yet advanced enough to confirm his theory.

He made other contributions to genetic research. He described what is known as Waardenburg syndrome, which is caused by a genetic mutation. The syndrome's symptoms include hearing loss (sometimes at birth) and changes in coloring of the hair, skin, and eyes. People with it may have different-colored eyes, one brown and one blue.

Chapter Two

Mistake
in Meiosis

One of the mysteries of Down syndrome was the fact that the odds of having a baby with the condition increase with the mother's age. Researchers say the number of Down syndrome births per one thousand babies born is five times higher for older women (thirty-five and older) than for younger women (twenty-five and younger).

For women under age twenty-five, the odds of having a baby with Down syndrome are about 1 in 1,500. By age thirty-five, the risk increases to somewhere between 1 in 300 and 1 in 400. By age forty, the odds may be as high as 1 in 100 to 1 in 50, and by the mid-forties, the rate can be as high as 1 in 25.

Before this mystery could be unraveled, however—indeed, before anything about genetic diseases could be understood—scientists had to solve the more general mystery of biological

Monk Gregor Mendel observed that offspring inherited traits not possessed by their parents. He concluded there are hereditary factors (genes) that are dominant and recessive.

inheritance. An important first step toward understanding this process occurred in 1866. That year, an Austrian monk named Gregor Mendel (1822–1884) published a scientific paper laying out the basic laws of genetics. This was the same year Down published his paper describing the syndrome that now bears his name. Mendel discovered these laws through a series of experiments with pea plants. He combined different varieties of pea plants that had distinct, easy-to-identify traits, such as height, shape, color, flower shape, and seed shape.

Down Syndrome

Mendel noticed that when he combined tall and short pea plants, he did not get medium-height offspring. Rather, the next generation included a certain percentage of tall plants and a certain percentage of short plants. When he combined light and dark pea plants, he didn't get plants with an in-between color. He got a certain percentage of light plants and a certain percentage of dark ones. When he combined plants that produced wrinkled seeds and plants that had smooth seeds, the result was the same—some wrinkled, some smooth, but none in between.

He also noted that sometimes the offspring of two short plants might be tall, but this was the case only if the short pea plants had tall ancestors. It seemed that pea plants, like human beings, could inherit a trait not present in their parents but present in the generations that preceded them.

Hidden Factors

Mendel concluded that hidden "heredity factors" were at work. These heredity factors determined whether the offspring would have the outward trait of the mother or the father. The trait could even remain hidden for a generation or two and then suddenly reappear. Mendel didn't know what the heredity factors looked like or how they worked, but he deduced that they existed based on his observations.

Today, we call these heredity factors genes. Genes, Mendel theorized, were what carried the information that made children resemble their parents. He proposed that genes did not change. The genes passed on to the child were exact copies of the ones the parents had inherited from their parents. And for each trait, there were two genes, one from each parent.

Gregor Mendel conducted his experiments on pea plants in this garden behind his abbey in Brno, Czech Republic.

Mendel had an answer for the question of why the combination of short and tall pea plants might produce a brood with some short offspring, some tall, but none of medium height. Genes, Mendel thought, were either "dominant" or "recessive." A dominant gene was always expressed over a recessive one. So a trait produced by a dominant gene always appeared in an offspring that had received a copy of that dominant gene. A child might inherit a recessive gene, and might even pass it on to the next generation, but this wouldn't make a difference in the child's appearance. The only reason we know that recessive genes exist is that sometimes a child inherits two of them. When there are two recessive genes for the same trait and no dominant genes to cancel them out, the recessive genes are expressed. Recessive genes explain why traits sometimes skip a generation.

CHARTING CHROMOSOMES

German scientist Walther Flemming (1843–1905) used dyes to study cells. He noticed a structure inside cells that strongly absorbed dye, and named it chromatin. He saw that right before cells divided, the chromatin separated into stringy objects. Other scientists would call these objects chromosomes. To describe the separation of the chromosomes, Flemming coined the term **mitosis**. He published his discoveries in 1882 in a book titled *Cell Substance, Nucleus, and Cell Division.*

In 1900, Dutch scientist Hugo de Vries (1848–1935) concluded the existence of the gene before he came across Mendel's historic paper. Then he discovered Flemming's work. Putting together the evidence, he realized that the chromosomes Flemming had observed were probably genetic material. He saw that in mitosis, two identical copies of the complete set of chromosomes moved to opposite sides of the cell, which then split and became two identical cells with the same genetic material.

Breakthrough

Nondisjunction is proved to be the cause of Down syndrome in 1959 by Jérôme Lejeune, Marthe Gautier, and M. Raymond Turpin.

Filling in the Blanks

Charles Darwin drew accurate conclusions despite lacking critical knowledge.

Charles Darwin made huge contributions to our understanding of biology. He was the first person to conclude that evolution depends on species being able to pass down variable traits to the next generations. These variable traits produce changes that can help a species survive. However, according to an article published by the Genetics Society of America (GSA), Darwin's theory of **natural selection** lacked one thing to make it complete.

He didn't understand how traits were inherited. He observed that populations in different locations that evolved from the same species of bird had developed new traits to help them adapt to their ecosystems (adaptive radiation). However, he did not know how those new traits were passed to future generations. It appears he believed in blended inheritance. An example of this would be a tall person and a short person having children of middle height. If all traits were blended in this way, eventually the variation within species would disappear. It's unfortunate that Darwin was not familiar with the work of contemporary botanist Gregor Mendel, who discovered the basics of heredity and published his results in 1866. Many scientific discoveries stayed hidden at the time because the tools of communication, such as today's Internet, weren't around to help spread them. If Darwin had known of Mendel's work, he could have used it to enhance his theory.

Natural selection fell out of favor and was discounted by early geneticists. They looked for mutations that created big changes. Subsequent studies went on to show natural selection in action, and Mendel's work on genetics was eventually rediscovered. When the revolutionary work of Mendel and Darwin was combined, the field of evolutionary biology took off. Darwin's principles, according to the GSA article, "now play a greater role in biology than ever before."

What was still needed was an explanation of how each parent contributes half of the offspring's genetic material, as Mendel stated, without giving the offspring a full complement of forty-six chromosomes.

DOUBLE DIVISION

German biologist August Weismann (1834–1914), in an 1892 book entitled *The Germ Plasm*, identified two types of cell division. One, mitosis, produces identical cells. This is what happens when our bodies grow. A skin cell or a muscle cell makes another one just like it. The second kind of cell division

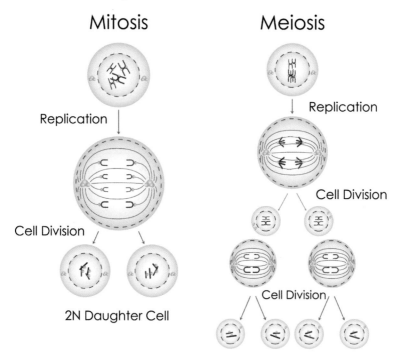

In mitosis, a cell copies itself and then divides, creating two identical daughter cells with a full set of chromosomes. In meiosis, the copied cells divide again, but this time the paired chromosomes separate. The result is four cells with half a set of chromosomes. These sex cells will join with another to form one cell with a complete set of chromosomes, half from each parent.

Down Syndrome

occurs when bodies produce reproductive cells—in human beings, the male sperm and the female egg, or **ovum**.

When our sex organs make reproductive cells, the chromosomes of a parent cell are copied. The new copy then splits in half and the chromosomes, which are ordinarily paired, undergo disjunction, or separation. In disjunction, half of the chromosomes go to one reproductive cell and half go to another. These cells then divide again. A human reproductive cell gets twenty-three chromosomes instead of forty-six. In males, each parent cell produces four sperm cells known as gametes. In females, one ovum is produced. The other cells don't contain enough cytoplasm and don't develop into an ovum. The entire process that results in reproductive cells with half the number of chromosomes as body cells is called **meiosis**. This is how each parent contributes only one of the two **genes** that determine each trait.

THE DOUBLE HELIX

By the 1940s, scientists knew each chromosome was made of a single long strand of a molecule they called **deoxyribonucleic acid (DNA)**. In the early 1950s, two young scientists, James D. Watson (1928–) and Francis Crick (1916–2004), achieved the greatest breakthrough in genetics since Mendel's original discoveries. They figured out the structure of the DNA molecule, what genes are made of, and how they are copied. Their work led to our understanding of how DNA influences the way living things grow and behave.

Watson and Crick built a model of DNA following the rules of chemical bonding. These rules state which atoms can form chemical bonds. Chemical analysis had shown which atoms were in a DNA molecule and in what proportions. Using this information, Watson and Crick constructed a three-dimensional model of a section of DNA. It explained how DNA works.

STEPS ON THE STAIRCASE

Watson and Crick's model describes DNA as a double-helix, a structure that resembles a spiral staircase. The steps of the staircase are pairs of chemical units called **nucleotides**. Each nucleotide is made up of a deoxyribose sugar molecule plus one of four bases—adenine, thymine, cytosine, or guanine.

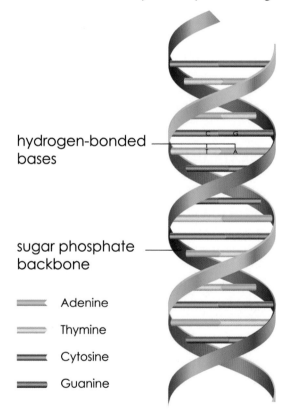

hydrogen-bonded bases

sugar phosphate backbone

Adenine
Thymine
Cytosine
Guanine

Nucleotides, the building blocks of DNA, contain three components: a phosphate, one of four bases, and one deoxyribose sugar. The DNA double helix is held together by a backbone of sugar molecules bonded by a phosphate. The bases line up in pairs–adenine with thymine; cytosine with guanine–and are held together by hydrogen bonds.

For simplicity, scientists refer to these nucleotides as A (adenine), T (thymine), C (cytosine), and G (guanine). These nucleotides can appear in any order in the DNA molecule.

Watson and Crick's model shows how DNA is copied. Each kind of nucleotide bonds with only one other kind of nucleotide. The adenine-containing nucleotide pairs with only the thymine-containing nucleotide, and the guanine-containing nucleotide fits with only the cytosine-containing nucleotide. So, A pairs only with T, and vice versa; C pairs only with G, and vice versa.

The model shows how, during both mitosis and meiosis, the DNA molecule "unzips." It splits lengthwise, leaving two halves of the DNA staircase made of the two opposite series of base pairs. Assisted by other molecules, each half of the DNA molecule becomes complete again. This results in the production of two complete DNA molecules—two copies of the original.

In his later work, Crick suggested that DNA was a code, a set of instructions written in the four nucleotides, A, T, C, and G. The chemical bases that formed the steps of the DNA staircase were like letters that spelled out sentences. The makeup of "sentences" determined the functions of the genes that contained them.

Each "sentence," or gene, with the help of other molecules in the cell, produces a protein. Genes are thus instructions for the way the body makes proteins. There are many kinds of proteins, each with its own job. Some are like building blocks, helping to form tissues like bone and muscle. Others are **enzymes**, organic molecules that speed chemical reactions. The many proteins that the genes code for are amazingly versatile and perform countless tasks within our bodies.

Cause of Down Syndrome

The process by which genes are handed down from parents to children is complex, with each step presenting a chance for an error. Errors during cell reproduction (meiosis) cause genetic diseases and disorders.

In 1932, Petrus Johannes Waardenburg suggested that Down syndrome might be caused by a problem during disjunction, when the pairs of chromosomes separate. Scientists had noticed that sometimes during disjunction, a pair of chromosomes could remain stuck together. Whenever this occurred, one reproductive cell did not get a copy of a particular chromosome, and another reproductive cell got two copies. The result would be a child who had either one less or one more chromosome than the usual number.

Waardenburg didn't have the equipment to prove his hypothesis. In the early 1950s, scientists developed new chemical solutions that made chromosomes condense and separate so that they were easier to count. In 1959, two scientists working separately—Jérôme Lejeune (1926–1994) in France, and Patricia Jacobs (1934–) in England—confirmed Waardenburg's theory about the probable cause of Down syndrome.

Three Causes, Same Result

People normally have forty-six chromosomes, but people with Down syndrome have forty-seven chromosomes. They have received an extra chromosome from one of their parents, usually the mother. There are three ways that a child can get the extra chromosome. In all three situations, the chromosome pair affected is the same—the one scientists label number 21.

Trisomy 21

Ninety-five percent of all cases of Down syndrome are caused by this condition, which physicians and scientists call **trisomy 21**, meaning three copies of chromosome 21. Instead of having two almost identical versions of chromosome 21, people with this kind of Down syndrome have three in every cell of their body.

Genes tell the body to produce proteins. Having an extra gene may mean that an extra amount of the protein will be produced. Too much of a given protein may upset the function of other proteins. In other cases, many different proteins combine to form large, complex structures in the cell. When that happens, the amount of the protein produced can make a difference in the cell's structure.

Translocation

About 3 to 4 percent of all cases of Down syndrome result from another chromosome defect called **translocation**. In this case, chromosome 21 attaches to another chromosome, forming a single chromosome. When the other chromosome involved is chromosome 14, the new combined chromosome is called t(14,21). (The other chromosomes that are sometimes involved are chromosomes 13, 15, and 22.) In this case, as a result of translocation, all the cells of the body have two copies of chromosome 21, one of chromosome 14, and one of t(14,21). Since, in effect, there is a complete extra set of chromosome 21 genes, the result is Down syndrome.

Translocation, like nondisjunction, just seems to be one of many possible errors that can occur during genetic copying. Translocation can affect any chromosome, but **embryos** that have translocation of chromosomes other than chromosome 21 become early miscarriages.

People who do not have outward signs of Down syndrome can still be carriers of translocation. Unaffected carriers have one copy each of chromosomes 21, 14, and t(14,21), but they have no extra chromosome 21, so they do not have Down syndrome. Unaffected carriers of t(14,21) are said to be "balanced" because they have the right number of each chromosome. If a mother (and only the mother) is a balanced carrier of t(14,21), there is about a 12 percent chance that her child will have Down syndrome. If the father (and only the father) is a balanced carrier, the chance that he will produce a child with Down syndrome is about 3 percent.

Mosaicism

About 1 to 2 percent of people with the disorder have a different and sometimes less severe version called **mosaic** Down syndrome. In mosaic Down syndrome, some cells of the body have trisomy 21—the extra chromosome 21—and some are normal. The genetic difference among the body's trillions of cells, like the differences in color among the pieces of a mosaic, suggested the name. Mosaicism can occur in two different, though related, ways.

In the first case, the trisomy 21 defect occurs when a fertilized egg begins to divide to become an embryo. The embryo is composed of identical cells called stem cells. These will later divide and become the specialized cells for all of the different parts of the body. In the course of the early series of cell divisions, disjunction fails, and one or more of the stem cells are affected. Only the body cells descended from these stem cells have the extra chromosome 21.

In the second case, the original fertilized egg has trisomy 21, but the disjunction error is naturally corrected in some of the stem cells. Some cells in the embryo have three copies of chromosome 21, and some cells have the usual two. Children with mosaicism have less severe cases of Down syndrome, scoring slightly higher on IQ tests.

Aging Problem

The reason older mothers have more children with Down syndrome has to do with the age of the ova (egg cells) produced by the mother. Human females produce all of their egg cells before they are born. An error during meiosis, such as nondisjunction, is more likely to occur in an ovum (a single egg cell) that has been stored in an ovary for forty-five years.

During each reproductive cycle, one to three ova start to reach maturity. The one that is the most mature is released during ovulation. If there is a disjunction error creating an extra chromosome 21 in that egg and it gets fertilized, the child will have Down syndrome.

Men do not produce all of their sperm cells before they are born. They make up to 1,500 every second. Older men produce more sperm cells with defective genetic material than do younger men. However, because millions of sperm compete to fertilize each egg, the odds are far lower that a damaged sperm cell will be the one that creates a new human life. Also, damaged sperm fade as they travel toward the egg, and are unlikely to complete the journey. Therefore, the age of the father is less of a factor than the age of the mother in producing children with Down syndrome.

Chapter Three

A Need
for Change

Lauren Potter is an actress with Down syndrome. Her most famous role is as the character Becky Johnson in the television series *Glee*. She has worked hard to achieve her dreams.

She has used her celebrity to inform people with disabilities who have been told "You can't" that "You can." She has also spoken out against bullying and the use of what she calls the R-word.

"The R-word is a hateful word. We need to stop, to end the R-word in every place," Potter said to the *Huffington Post* in 2015. "I don't know why people are so mean. All I want from you is to stop saying the R-word ... That's what I am trying to let my fans know, that's a really bad word. You can't say anything bad about other people—it will hurt other people."

Lauren Potter has exposed the wrongdoing of imposing limits on people with Down syndrome in her role as Becky Johnson in *Glee*.

Potter knows from experience. "I was bullied when I was a kid," Potter told the *Hays Daily News*. "I was pushed down, made to eat sand, called the R-word. That's why I have been fighting to end bullying."

ATTITUDE ADJUSTMENT

The fight to change attitudes about people with Down syndrome has been going on for decades. In the 1940s and 1950s, millions of mothers and mothers-to-be looked to the best-selling book *Baby and Child Care* for guidance on child rearing. Written by Dr. Benjamin Spock (1903–1998), the

Dr. Benjamin Spock influenced a generation of parents, but he proved to be wrong about raising children with Down syndrome.

book advised that babies born with Down syndrome should immediately be institutionalized. That is, they should be sent to live in a hospital-like facility where professionals would care for them. "If the infant exists at a level that is hardly human," Spock wrote, "it is much better for the other children and parents to have him cared for elsewhere."

Spock's advice followed what most doctors believed at the time. We now know, however, that Spock and his fellow pediatricians were wrong. Later advancements in the treatment of children with Down syndrome proved that they are quite sociable and suffer psychologically when they are institutionalized. The mid-twentieth-century approach to Down syndrome—separating the children from their families, and separating them from other children—was as mistaken as John Langdon Down's theory that his patients were throwbacks to some prehistoric common ancestor of Europeans and Asians. The results of this attitude were tragic for the children with Down syndrome, who generally received care that was inferior to the care they would have received at home. It was also difficult for the parents, who had to live with the guilt of abandoning a child.

🧬 Breakthrough

In 1961, researchers discover mosaicism, a form of Down syndrome in which not all cells in a person's body have an extra chromosome 21.

No Place Like Home

Like other children, children with Down syndrome are happiest and healthiest living in a loving home. Like other children, they also need stimulation and a variety of social contact. Research shows that children with Down syndrome growing up in families progress faster and achieve more than children with the disorder growing up in institutions. Professionals, no matter how well trained, are not better than family members at caring for children. Research also shows that children with Down syndrome who are **mainstreamed** (put in regular classes with children without disabilities) progress at a faster rate and achieve more than children with Down syndrome who learn in special-education settings.

Degree of Difficulty

The mainstreaming of students with Down syndrome has created an outbreak of educational firsts. Here are some of the inspiring stories:

» Ezra Roy graduated magna cum laude from Texas Southern University in December 2014. He was the first student with Down syndrome to graduate from a four-year university without special education classes. His mother left the family

Placing children with Down syndrome in classes with children who don't have a disability is called mainstreaming. This practice has allowed many children with Down syndrome to reach their intellectual capacity and to exceed educational expectations.

when he was two, and he was raised by his father.
Alvin Roy taught his son how to paint using alternative
techniques, and this helped develop the young man's manual
dexterity and his cognitive function.

» Megan McCormick graduated with honors with an associate's
degree in education from Bluegrass Technical and Community
College in Kentucky in 2013. She is the first person with her
condition to get a two-year degree in the state's history. She
wants to work at the kindergarten and elementary level as a
para-educator to honor all of those who helped her.

» It took twelve years, but Angela Long of Michigan earned
an associate's degree in liberal arts from Schoolcraft College
in 2014. She paid for her education by working at Kroger, a
grocery store.

» Ryan Burke graduated from Notre Dame College Prep in
Niles, Illinois, in 2013. He participated in the marching band,
on the swim team, and on the student council. Because of
Ryan's success and the drive of his parents, Notre Dame
became one of the few Catholic schools in the country with
a structured program for students with special needs.

Studies and surveys also have something to say about the experience of the families of children with Down syndrome. Raising a child with Down syndrome is a profound challenge, bringing special worries about the child's health, education, and his or her future. These worries generally do not destroy families or weaken them, however.

This is not to deny that it is difficult to raise a child with a lifelong health problem or disability. Children and adults with Down syndrome often have an impaired immune system and may frequently become ill. Despite improvements in medical treatment, many people with Down syndrome die in childhood or in early youth, usually because of heart defects. Raising a child who is ill and who may die young can be a terrible ordeal for families, but many parents have met the challenge with a positive attitude.

STILL A PROBLEM

The perspective of some people toward Down syndrome still hasn't evolved. In 2014, a well-known biologist said it would be immoral to bring a child with Down syndrome into the world. Two educators with backgrounds in science rebutted this statement with facts about children with Down syndrome in an opinion column published in the *New York Times*. The educators wrote that research found the following:

- Parents of preschoolers with Down syndrome suffered less stress than parents with an autistic child.
- The divorce rate in families with a child with Down syndrome was lower than in families with children with other developmental disabilities or no disabilities.

- Eighty-eight percent of siblings said they were better people because a younger sibling had Down syndrome.
- Of children with Down syndrome over the age of twelve, 99 percent said they were happy with their lives.
- People with Down syndrome have adaptive skills, which measure the ability of a person to adapt to their environment, that are higher than expected of someone with their IQ.

DIFFERENT NEEDS

Children and adults with Down syndrome have different needs, different personalities, and different potential for achievement in life. Some are self-confident and outgoing and have active social lives. Some are drawn to sports, engaging and excelling in swimming, gymnastics, water skiing, or riding. Others are placid and shy, preferring quiet activities with a few friends.

Babies with Down syndrome grow and develop at a slower pace than other babies. They tend to reach developmental milestones later than other children. For instance, a child who develops normally usually learns to walk at twelve to fourteen months. A child with Down syndrome, on the other hand, might learn to walk between eighteen and thirty-six months. Similarly, first words and sentences will come later than with other children.

Some people with Down syndrome have intellectual abilities that are within the normal range; the majority have a moderate degree of intellectual disability. The lifestyles that people with Down syndrome lead depend on innate physical differences and differences of ability. They also depend, to a great degree, on the support they get from both professionals and family. Children with Down syndrome often attend regular schools in regular classes, with differing levels of support. Most young people with Down syndrome graduate from high school. Some are enrolled in postsecondary educational programs, including colleges and vocational programs. Like the rest of us, people with Down syndrome continue to learn and progress throughout their lives.

Strong parental support can help children with Down syndrome develop and go on to lead productive lives.

Many adults with Down syndrome have jobs. Some work in special settings designed for people with disabilities. Others hold jobs they find themselves on the open labor market. Adults

Down Syndrome

with Down syndrome live in a variety of settings—by themselves or with roommates in apartments, condominiums, or houses; in special facilities called group homes that have support services; or with family members.

It is not uncommon for people with Down syndrome to marry. Often, their spouses have Down syndrome, too. Based on the available statistics, the National Down Syndrome Society reports that about 50 percent of women with the disorder are fertile, or able to have children. Approximately half of the children born to mothers with Down syndrome also have the disorder or some other developmental disability. Men with Down syndrome can father children.

People with Down syndrome have normal emotional and physical needs, and except for lower rates of fertility their reproductive functioning is the same as for nondisabled people. It is thus important that they receive sexual education tailored to their intellectual abilities, and that they learn appropriate behavior and self-assertion skills so they don't become victims of abuse.

Chapter Four

Improved Environment

Andy Gardiner became president of the Florida senate in 2014. He and his wife, Camille, are parents of Andrew Jr., a child with Down syndrome who was born in 2004. Gardiner combined his jobs as father and senator by backing bills that reflect the desire to raise his son as he and his wife would any other child. Andy and Camille expect achievement and independence from Andrew Jr.

The bills, which could put Florida in the lead in such matters, would create tax-free savings accounts for the disabled to help them after their parents are gone, allow universities to set up courses focusing on career readiness for students with intellectual disabilities, and greatly increase funding for vouchers for special education students. As of 2015, these measures had not yet been officially passed.

Florida senator Andy Gardiner took his then eight-year-old son Andrew to the opening day of the 2012 legislative session in Tallahassee.

Efforts such as this are part of the changing environment for people with Down syndrome. Over the years, better care, better education, and medical advances have dramatically improved the mental functioning and general health of people with Down syndrome. The life expectancy of a person with the disorder is nearly five times what it was sixty-plus years ago. According to the US Centers for Disease Control and Prevention (CDC), the average life expectancy rose to forty-seven in 2007, up from about ten in 1960. By 2015, the life expectancy of a person with Down syndrome had risen to almost sixty.

The future holds promise for even more fundamental improvements in the lives of people with Down syndrome. So far, though, the most important changes that have occurred are the result of major shifts in public attitudes. These shifts are part of a general revolution in the approach to individuals with disabilities in our society.

Advances in medical science have improved the physical and mental health of people with Down syndrome. Medical science is also the key to testing whether unborn children have Down syndrome.

A new test, called a cell-free DNA test, recently went through trials on sixteen thousand women. It was found to be far more accurate in finding trisomy 21 than previous tests and it delivered far fewer false positives. False positives indicate a problem is present when it isn't. Even with these accurate results, all positive tests should be followed at a later date by other tests that can confirm the diagnosis.

One other benefit of the tests, which were not approved as of the spring of 2015, is that they can be administered as early as ten weeks into the pregnancy. The test picks up free-floating DNA from the **fetus**, and it can find extra copies of chromosome 21 and other genetic conditions.

OTHER OPTIONS

Blood tests for Down syndrome are performed between the fourteenth and sixteenth week of pregnancy. These tests check the levels of certain proteins and **hormones** (chemical messengers). The proteins and hormones are present in greater quantities when the fetus has Down syndrome. About 60 to 80 percent of Down syndrome cases can be detected with fetal blood tests.

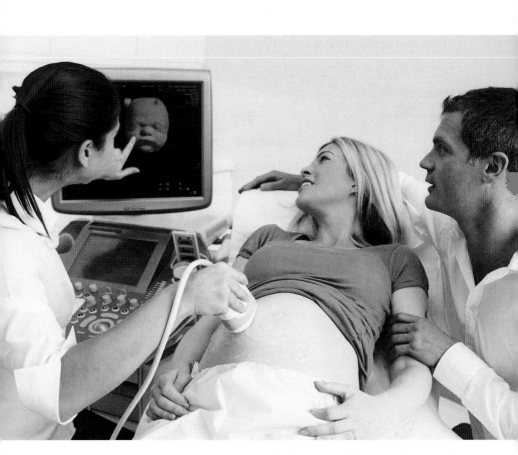

A 3-D ultrasound can provide a detailed view of a developing child in its mother's womb.

An **ultrasound** examination is another test performed in almost all pregnancies in developed countries today. It is a low-risk procedure. An ultrasound uses high-frequency sound waves to create real-time, moving images of the inside of the body. Ultrasound images can be in three dimensions and seen on a monitor. During ultrasound exams, physicians look for physical indications of Down syndrome. These include a thickening of the skin at the back of the neck, bright spots on the kidneys or heart, short arms or legs, or reduced head size. If any of these physical markers are observed, other testing is generally recommended.

Advancements in Down Syndrome

1866 Gregor Mendel publishes his findings on the principles of heredity; John Langdon Down publishes the first thorough clinical description of individuals with Down syndrome.

1932 Petrus Waardenburg guesses that Down syndrome may be the result of a chromosomal defect caused by nondisjunction, the failure of a pair of chromosomes to separate during meiosis.

1944 Oswald Theodore Avery (1877–1955) and his coworkers describe DNA (deoxyribonucleic acid) as the hereditary material.

1953 James D. Watson and Francis Crick describe the double-helix structure of DNA.

1959 Jérôme Lejeune, Marthe Gautier, and M. Raymond Turpin confirm the hypothesis that claims Down syndrome is caused by nondisjunction.

1960 The National Association for Down Syndrome is founded.

1967 C. B. Jacobson and R. H. Barter use **amniocentesis** for the first time in a **prenatal** diagnosis of a genetic disorder.

1970 Hamilton Smith, at Johns Hopkins University, discovers **restriction enzymes**. These are "molecular scissors" that protect bacteria by cutting the DNA in invading viruses.

1975   Edward Southern develops a method to isolate and analyze fragments of DNA.

1979   The National Down Syndrome Society is founded in New York City.

1987   A gene associated with **Alzheimer's disease** is found on chromosome 21, suggesting a link with Down syndrome.

2000   The Chromosome 21 Mapping and Sequencing Consortium publishes the gene sequence of chromosome 21 in the magazine *Nature*.

2003   In April, the International Human Genome Sequencing Consortium publishes the full sequence of the entire **human genome**.

2010   Tests for evaluating cognition in Down syndrome patients are validated in August. The Arizona Cognitive Test Battery is needed to standardize measurements of how much cognition-enhancing drugs are helping.

2010   The Anna and John J. Sie Center for Down Syndrome opens in Colorado in November and accepts patients from throughout the world.

If the risk of Down syndrome—or any other genetic disorder—is considered high, a procedure called amniocentesis may be performed, usually around the sixteenth week of pregnancy. Amniocentesis involves testing **amniotic fluid**, the liquid in which the fetus is suspended. First, an ultrasound examination is done to show the location of the amniotic cavity and the fetus. Then, a needle is inserted into the amniotic cavity through the mother's abdomen, and a small amount of amniotic fluid is drawn up through the needle. The amniotic fluid contains cells from the fetus. These cells are cultured— that is, grown—and then they are tested for chromosomal abnormalities. It usually takes between twelve and twenty days to obtain the results.

Breakthrough

The gene sequence of chromosome 21 is published in 2000. This smallest of chromosomes is the second to be deciphered.

Amniocentesis is a relatively accurate predictor of Down syndrome, but it is a risky procedure. It can lead to infection, bleeding, or cramping. The needle can also accidentally puncture the skin of the fetus. Amniocentesis causes miscarriage about one out of every five hundred times it is performed.

PARENTAL SUPPORT

People who learn their unborn child has Down syndrome have support and information they didn't have in the past. In a study conducted in the late 1980s, all sixteen parents surveyed reported that raising a child with Down syndrome had a profound impact

Older siblings report that having a brother or sister with Down syndrome makes them better people.

on their lives. All reported that the positive aspects outweighed the negative. Parents in this study said that having a child with Down syndrome had brought the family closer together, taught them the meaning of unconditional love, "put things in perspective," and taught them the importance of diversity.

As one parent interviewed for the study put it, as quoted in *Genetic Disease*, "At the time [of the diagnosis], you feel that this is the biggest tragedy that ever happened. If we could have known what it would be like to have M., we wouldn't have been nearly so sad. No one really mentioned the positive side."

Melanie McLaughlin, a filmmaker from Boston, told ABC News in 2009 that after the shock of receiving a Down syndrome diagnosis she contacted the Parents First Call program. It is sponsored by the Massachusetts Down Syndrome Congress.

First Call gets expecting parents in touch with a family raising a child with Down syndrome and it gives them accurate information about the condition and the children who have it. McLaughlin said she got to meet a five-year-old girl with the syndrome and this helped rid her of misconceptions of what life would be like as a parent of such a child.

"She played hide-and-seek, and she kept jumping out, telling us where she was hiding," McLaughlin told ABC News of her encounter. "She was amazing. I was thinking she would be sitting in a chair unresponsive and drooling. Actually, she was much like our other children."

The National Down Syndrome Society provides contact information where expecting parents in other states can get needed support.

Chapter Five

Rapid Advancements

Life has changed for the better for people born with an extra copy of chromosome 21, and medical science is on the path to making it better still. These latest cutting-edge advances have not yet been approved, but they hold great promise.

Dr. Brian Skotko is a medical geneticist and the co-director of the Down Syndrome Program at Massachusetts General Hospital. He is also the brother of a woman with Down syndrome. Among the things he is researching is a drug called scyllo-inositol, which is being made and tested by Transition Therapeutic. The drug was intended to treat Alzheimer's disease. It prevents the buildup of beta-amyloid plaques, which is common in Alzheimer's patients, and it improves working memory. The formation of these plaques is "encoded by genes located on chromosome 21," Skotko told CBS News.

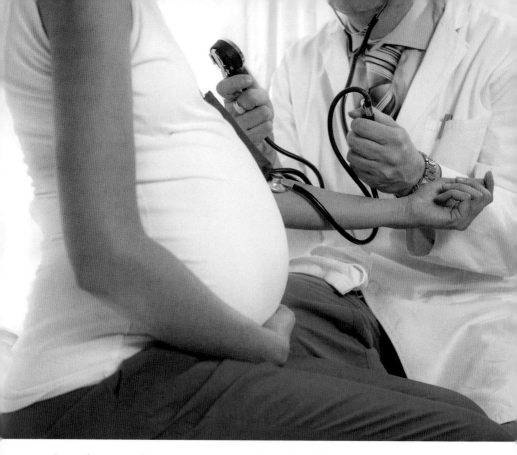

Researchers are working on ways to improve the intellectual development of children with Down syndrome before they are born.

This and another drug being tested in 2015 could help cognition in Down syndrome patients now and delay the onset of Alzheimer's, which affects them at earlier ages than it does people in the general population.

Tests are also being done on a pill that a pregnant woman would take to help increase brain development in unborn children with Down syndrome. The pill would contain huge amounts of antioxidants obtained from fruits and leafy vegetables. Brain cells die, and are never replaced, due to oxidative stress. It is hoped these pills will relieve the stress, rescue those brain cells, and improve brain function in children with Down syndrome.

Down Syndrome

Tests on mice produced some positive results. As of 2015, tests on humans were years away, but if they work, this treatment would be the first to come in pill form.

The biggest advances in treating genetic diseases have come in gene therapy. People with Down syndrome have an extra copy of chromosome 21, so research has focused on finding the functions of the genes on chromosome 21, a great challenge. The chromosome contains 33.8 million nucleotide base pairs of DNA. Scientists estimate that these 33.8 million DNA base pairs probably contain the code for fewer than three hundred genes. These are the genes that need to be precisely located on the chromosome to know which ones are involved in Down syndrome and how they interact.

PROTEIN OVERLOAD

The job of certain genes is to instruct the body to make a particular protein. An extra copy of a gene leads the body to make too much of that protein. Getting instructions from three genes instead of two, the body with Down syndrome produces more of a given protein, perhaps as much as 50 percent more. The results are complicated because proteins do so many things in the human body and there are so many types of proteins.

Enzymes, for example, are proteins that make chemical reactions happen. Structural proteins are the building blocks of our body; they make up our hearts, lungs, bones, and skin. Hormones are proteins that act as chemical messengers, carrying signals between our cells. Receptor proteins make our senses work. The proteins actin and myosin make our heart and skeletal muscles move. The immune system helps the body fight off

Down Syndrome Fact Sheet

» Down syndrome occurs when an individual has an extra full or partial copy of chromosome 21.

» There are three types of Down syndrome: trisomy 21, translocation, and mosaicism.

» Down syndrome is the most commonly occurring chromosomal condition. There are more than four hundred thousand people living with Down syndrome in the United States.

» One in every 691 babies in the United States is born with Down syndrome.

» People with Down syndrome have an increased risk for certain medical conditions such as congenital heart defects, respiratory and hearing problems, Alzheimer's disease, childhood leukemia, and thyroid conditions.

» Alzheimer's hits people with Down syndrome between the ages of thirty and thirty-five; it starts in most others between the ages of fifty and seventy-five.

» A few of the common physical traits of Down syndrome are low muscle tone, small stature, an upward slant to the eyes, and a single deep crease across the center of the palm.

» Life expectancy for people with Down syndrome has increased from twenty-five in 1983 to sixty in 2014.

» Most or all people with Down syndrome also suffer from sleep apnea. This could contribute to many of the problems associated with the condition, such as impaired cognitive ability.

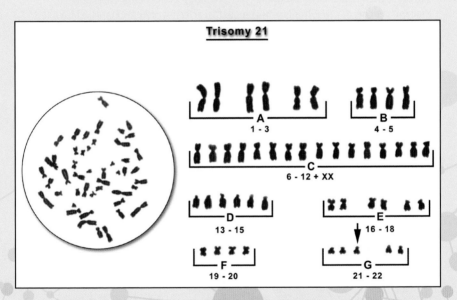

This collage of digital images taken through a microscope shows the karyotype of a person with trisomy 21, the main cause of Down syndrome. A karyotype is a complete set of chromosomes. Chromosomes are paired, but in trisomy 21, there is a third copy of chromosome 21.

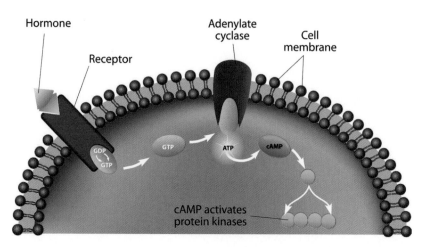

When a hormone plugs into its receptor on a cell, the regulatory enzyme GTP is released. The GTP is itself regulated by adenylate cyclase, which produces cyclic adenosine monophosphate, or cAMP. This is a messenger that activates protein kinases, which affect protein function. These proteins have many effects on the body, and too many of them can lead to problems such as Down syndrome.

infection with proteins. Even DNA itself, which encodes the orders to produce proteins, is regulated by proteins called DNA-binding proteins.

All these proteins interact with each other in a complex way, so the overproduction of even one of them has unpredictable results.

Novel Approach

Jeanne Lawrence, a researcher in pediatrics and developmental biology at the University of Massachusetts Medical School, has proposed taking a step beyond gene therapy. She wants to do chromosome therapy. This will involve turning off the extra chromosome in children with Down syndrome so it won't generate the extra proteins. In this way, doctors could stop Down syndrome before it can get started.

Down Syndrome

The method she and her fellow researchers want to use is already used by the human body. Females have two X chromosomes. Somewhere in our evolutionary development, women's bodies have added a genetic element that turns off one of the two X chromosomes. The chromosome stays on the genome, but it doesn't actually work. In this way, females don't get too much of whatever the chromosome produces.

In an isolated laboratory setting, researchers have been able to deactivate the extra chromosome 21. This groundbreaking work is being funded by the National Institutes of Health. There are many hurdles and a lot of work to be done before this treatment can be used on unborn children. However, it promises to have a profound effect on the treatment of Down syndrome.

Breakthrough

A new mouse model for studying Down syndrome is created in 2005 by inserting a human chromosome 21 into mouse cells. This allows scientists to see how some genes affect the condition.

GLOSSARY

Alzheimer's disease • A degenerative disease of the central nervous system that leads to premature senile mental deterioration.

amniocentesis • The surgical insertion of a hollow needle through the abdominal wall and into the uterus of a pregnant woman to obtain amniotic fluid, usually in order to detect a possible chromosomal abnormality in the fetus.

amniotic fluid • The fluid in which an embryo is suspended.

chromosome • A structure containing most or all of an organism's genes; humans normally have forty-six chromosomes.

deoxyribonucleic acid (DNA) • The molecules inside cells that carry genetic information and pass it from one generation to the next.

embryo • An unborn human or animal in the early stages of growth.

enzymes • Proteins produced by the body that greatly accelerate the rate of specific biochemical reactions.

fetus • A developing human, usually from three months after conception to birth.

gene • A length of DNA (a series of nucleotides) on a chromosome; the functional unit of inheritance.

genetic disorder • A disease linked to the basic processes of biological inheritance.

heredity • The passing of physical or mental attributes genetically from one generation to the next.

hormone • A product of living cells that circulates in the body and produces a specific effect on cells far from its point of origin.

human genome • The full collection of genes needed to produce a human being.

mainstream • To educate a student with a disability in a class with students without disabilities.

meiosis • A type of cell division, necessary for reproduction, which produces four cells, each with half of the chromosomes of the parent cell.

mitosis • A type of cell division that results in two cells that have the same number of chromosomes as the parent cell.

mongolism • An early name for Down syndrome; it is no longer used to describe the condition and is generally considered offensive.

mosaicism • A condition in which different cells of the body have different genetic makeups.

natural selection • The process by which organisms better adapt to their environment so they can survive and produce more offspring. When adapted species live and others become extinct, this is known as survival of the fittest.

nondisjunction • The failure of a pair of chromosomes to separate during cell division; the major cause of trisomy 21, which results in Down syndrome.

nucleotide • A subunit of DNA or RNA that consists of a nitrogenous base, a phosphate molecule, and a sugar molecule. Thousands of nucleotides are linked to form a DNA or an RNA molecule.

ovum (plural **ova**) • A female sex cell, which contains half the genetic material the offspring will receive.

pathology • The study of the causes and effects of illnesses; something that is creating a health condition.

prenatal • Prior to birth.

restriction enzymes • Enzymes that break DNA into fragments at specific sites.

translocation • A chromosomal abnormality in which a part of a chromosome is transferred to a nonhomologous (dissimilar) chromosome; sometimes a cause of Down syndrome.

trisomy 21 • The condition of having an extra chromosome 21; the principle cause of Down syndrome.

ultrasound • A diagnostic procedure that uses high-frequency sound waves to produce two-dimensional or three-dimensional images for the assessment of internal body structures.

Websites

The Mayo Clinic.
www.mayoclinic.org/diseases-conditions/down-syndrome/basics/causes/
con-20020948
One of the leading medical research facilities in the United States shares
its knowledge on Down syndrome, including information on risk factors,
complications, and how to cope and find support.

The Tech Museum of Innovation: Ask a Geneticist
genetics.thetech.org/ask/ask157
This Stanford-backed site provides a wealth of facts and a forum for asking
questions about genetics.

WebMD
www.webmd.com/children/tc/down-syndrome-topic-overview
This reliable source of information provides a one-stop guide, from the causes
and symptoms of the condition, to videos and links to the latest news.

Organizations

Down Syndrome Research Foundation
1409 Sperling Avenue
Burnaby, BC V5B 4J8
Canada
(604) 444-3773
www.dsrf.org

National Down Syndrome Society
666 Broadway, 8th Floor
New York, NY 10012
(800) 221-4602
www.ndss.org

FOR FURTHER READING

Daugherty, Paul. *An Uncomplicated Life: A Father's Memoir of His Exceptional Daughter*. New York: William Morrow, 2015.

DK. *The Science Book*. Big Ideas Simply Explained. London: DK, 2014.

Hamilton, Janet. *James Watson: Solving the Mystery of DNA*. Nobel Prize–Winning Scientists. Berkeley Heights, NJ: Enslow, 2004.

Hulings, Kathryn U. *Life with a Superhero: Raising Michael Who Has Down Syndrome*. Denton, TX: University of North Texas Press, 2013.

Kidder, Cynthia S., and Brian Skotko. *Common Threads: Celebrating Life With Down Syndrome*. Rochester Hills, MI: Band of Angels Press, 2007.

Krasnow, David. *Genetics*. Discovery Channel School Science. New York: Gareth Stevens Publishing, 2003.

Mooney, Carla. *Genetics: Breaking the Code of Your DNA*. Inquire and Investigate. White River Junction, VT: Nomad Press, 2014.

Robinson, Tara Rodden. *Genetics for Dummies*. Hoboken, NJ: Wiley, 2010.

SELECTED BIBLIOGRAPHY

Publications

Capone, George T. "Down Syndrome: Genetic Insights and Thoughts on Early Intervention." *Infants & Young Children* 17, no. 1 (January–March 2004): pp. 45–58.

Cohen, William I., Lynne Nadel, and Myra E. Madnick, eds. *Down Syndrome: Visions for the 21st Century*. New York, NY: Wiley-Liss, 2002.

Hawley, R. Scott, and Catherine A. Mori. *The Human Genome: A User's Guide*. 3rd ed. New York, NY: Academic Press, 2011.

Rainer, John D., ed. *Genetic Disease: The Unwanted Inheritance*. Binghamton, NY: Haworth Press, 1989.

Shapiro, Robert. *The Human Blueprint: The Race to Unlock the Secrets of Our Genetic Script*. New York, NY: St. Martin's Press, 1991.

Van Riper, Marcia. "Living with Down Syndrome." *Down Syndrome Quarterly* 4, no. 1 (March 1999): pp. 1–11.

Online Articles

Buxton, Ryan. "'Glee' Star Has 1 Request For Fans: Stop Using The
'R-Word'" *The Huffington Post*, February 2, 2015. Accessed April 14,
2015. www.huffingtonpost.com/2015/02/02/glee-actress-lauren-potter-r-
word_n_6581562.html

Edgin, Jamie, and Fabian Fernandez. "The Truth About Down Syndrome."
New York Times, August 28, 2014. Accessed April 13, 2015. www.
nytimes.com/2014/08/29/opinion/the-truth-about-down-syndrome.
html?_r=0

James, Susan Donaldson. "Down Syndrome Births Are Down in U.S." ABC
News, November 2, 2009. Accessed April 14, 2015. www.abcnews.
go.com/Health/w_ParentingResource/down-syndrome-births-drop-us-
women-abort/story?id=8960803

March, William. "Senator's Child With Down Syndrome Inspires
Legislation." Associated Press, April 7, 2015. Accessed April 14, 2015.
www.news-press.com/story/news/politics/2015/04/06/senators-child-
syndrome-inspires-legislation/25391449/

Techonomy. "Hope Seen in Chromosome Therapy for Down Syndrome."
Forbes Magazine, November 10, 2013. Accessed April 17, 2015. www.
forbes.com/sites/techonomy/2013/11/10/hope-seen-in-chromosome-
therapy-for-down-syndrome/

Index

Page numbers in **boldface** are illustrations. Entries in **boldface** are glossary terms.